STATE vs. PARENTS

FAITH AND FREEDOM
SERIES

STATE VS. PARENTS

THREATS TO RAISING YOUR CHILDREN

JOHN W. WHITEHEAD

MOODY PRESS
CHICAGO

© 1995 by
JOHN W. WHITEHEAD

All rights reserved.
No part of this book may be reproduced
in any form without permission
in writing from the publisher,
except in the case of brief quotations
embodied in critical articles or reviews.

All Scripture quotations, unless indicated,
are from the *Holy Bible: New International
Version*®. NIV®. Copyright © 1973, 1978, 1984
International Bible Society. Used by
permission of Zondervan Publishing House.
All rights reserved.

ISBN: 0-8024-6682-6

1 3 5 7 9 10 8 6 4 2

Printed in the United States of America

For most Americans, the term "family values" is simply a political term that has recently become part of the unique American lexicon. Many liberal politicians decry the term as merely a euphemism for racism and class discrimination. On the other side, many conservatives use the term as a catchall concept to rationalize the moral and financial crises in which America finds itself today. Many simply have no idea what the term implies. Still others have no interest in the subject and believe that the issue has no relevance to their lives.

While the rhetoric continues, the status and respect for the family as a critical social and governmental unit continues to disappear, and nothing much is being done about it. Many government agencies, including the courts, continue to undermine the family as a social unit and promulgate programs and policies that are actively hostile to the traditional family configuration.[1]

Many who have not yet lifted their fingers against the pressures of the government's burdens on the family are wholly unaware of the true state of family values, and the value of the traditional family, in our nation. Many others are too painfully aware.

The purpose of this booklet is to discuss the current status of the family and parental rights in the United States. Thus, the historical importance of the traditional family structure and the deference paid to the sacred rights of parents, as well as the erosion of these concepts, will be reviewed. The state's control over children, and thus families, will then be discussed in the context of diminished parental rights. Next, the emerging concept of children's rights will be discussed, and the reasons behind this state of affairs will be posed. Finally, practical suggestions regarding the revitalization of the family, and thus parental rights, will be made.

The Autonomous Family

America's Founders showed great deference to the role of the family in the new nation. Thus, many of the basic functions of society in the early days of America were carried out by independent families, not the federal government:

> Relative to family life, the genius of the American Constitution of 1787 lay in its avoidance of ideology and its devotion to authentic federal principle. Family issues of marriage, divorce, children, inheritance, education, mutual support, and welfare were not questions for the new federal govern-

6

ment. They were questions reserved to the states, where Christian conceptions of patriarchy, charity, and shared obligation and common law understandings of family and community governance could, and did, hold sway.[2]

The family was, as a court noted in 1952, also viewed as important for moral and practical reasons:

> The family is the basic unit of our society, the center of the personal affections that ennoble and enrich human life. It channels biological drives that might otherwise become socially destructive; it ensures the care and education of children in a stable environment; it establishes continuity from one generation to another; it nurtures and develops the individual initiative that distinguishes a free people.[3]

During the last hundred years or so, the state has increasingly taken from the family, and thus from parents, the responsibility for nurturing and developing "the individual initiative that distinguishes a free people." Today, the notion of the state's responsibility has become so embedded in the culture that many parents *give* this responsibility to the state in exchange for state "benefits" and *demand* that the state assume responsibility for their children's education and welfare.

No longer the unquestioned building block of American society, the autonomous family functioning under Judeo-Christian principles has given way, both legally and culturally, to so-called organizational preferences, or voluntary groupings prompted by sexual orientation, convenience, and transitory desires.

But without the autonomous family and its *permanent and insoluble lifetime commitments*, democratic self-rule and ultimately civilized society will cease to exist. In her essay "Dan Quayle Was Right," Barbara DaFoe Whitehead discusses this prospect:

> The founding of the United States set in motion a new political order based to an unprecedented degree on individual rights, personal choice, and egalitarian relationships. Since then these values have spread beyond their original domain of political relationships to define social relationships as well. During the past twenty-five years these values have had a particularly profound impact on the family.

> Increasingly, political principles of individual rights and choice shape our understanding of family commitment and solidarity. Family relationships are viewed not as permanent or binding but as *voluntary* and *easily terminable*. Moreover, the family loses its central importance as an institution in civil society, accomplishing certain social goals such as raising children and caring for its members, and becomes a means to achieving greater individual happiness—*a lifestyle choice*.

> More than a century and a half ago Alexis de Tocqueville made the observation that an individualistic society

depends on a communitarian institution like the family for its continued existence. The family cannot be constituted like the liberal state, nor can it be governed entirely by that state's principles. Yet the family serves as the seedbed for the virtues required by a liberal state. The family is responsible for teaching lessons of independence, self-restraint, responsibility, and right conduct, which are essential to a free, democratic society. If the family fails in these tasks, then the entire experiment in democratic self-rule is jeopardized.[4]

The Child Savers

Critics of a society founded on traditional family structures have long condemned the institution of the family and the claim of sacred and natural family rights.[5] For these critics, the family stands for and perpetuates only a parochial self-interest. If social equality is ever to be achieved, the critics say, the family must be abolished and, with it, its accompanying social classes. Some radical feminists have declared the traditional family structure as nothing more than the perpetuation of male dominance and a place for acquiring female acquiescence to such dominance. Various other theorists argue that, in place of child rearing by parents who allegedly lack training and a sense of communal responsibility, the state should intervene in child rearing on the basis of an egalitarian social agenda. Thus, by abolishing the traditional family, conditions of equality may be better effected and the public interest served.[6] The currently popular African proverb has become, in many ways, the slogan for this view: "It takes an entire village to raise a child."

Thus, the American "Child Saving Movement" which began in the mid-1800s sought termination of parental rights for the sake of child welfare. But the movement failed to distinguish the important difference between children who were *poor* and children who were *neglected and/or delinquent*. As these so-called child advocates argued: "May not the natural parents, when unequal to the task of education or unworthy of it, be supplanted by the *parens patriae*, or common guardianship of the community?"[7]

Joining with the social workers and the "progressive spirit," the child savers attacked the shield of "natural" parental rights and began the juvenile justice system:

> "Parents could no longer shield themselves behind natural rights," one early enthusiast said. Without a formal hearing or other consideration of due process, hundreds of thousands of American children would be seized by the Child Savers and incarcerated in reform or "industrial" schools, all for "the welfare of the child," a lone actor in an individualistic world.[8]

From this position, "late 19th century proponents of mandatory state schooling, for example, ridiculed attention to the sacred rights and privileges of parents. Court decisions on mandatory attendance laws ruled that the principle of *parens patriae* took precedence over the rights of parents."[9]

By 1930, the "parenting state" had emerged and labeled "Uncle Sam's Child" as a human being "who belongs to the community almost as much as to the family, a 'new racial experiment,' and a citizen of a 'world predestinedly moving toward unity.'"[10]

Although the American family idealized by television's model families, the Nelsons and Cleavers, reappeared during the brief period from 1946 to 1961,[11] its appearance was sustained even this short time, according to one commentator, only by America's distraction by the post-World War II economic boom and anti-Communist frenzy.[12] Thus:

> This halcyon age collapsed in the 1960s
> ... and the old trends and their parasitical "professions" came roaring back. Marriage rates tumbled while divorce rates soared. Illegitimacy spread rapidly among white Americans (it was already common among blacks), while marital fertility collapsed. The "sexual revolution" came out from under the covers, where it had been heating up since the American libido was drafted in 1942 to do battle with the arthritic and thinning legions of Christian decency. The family itself fell into disrepute, pummeled by neo-Malthusians, neofeminists, neo-Marxists, and neo-pagans alike.[13]

11

The disappearance of America's autonomous families quickened: divorce, the sexual revolution, the women's liberation movement, and technology were taking their toll. According to an article in *The Atlantic Monthly*, in the postwar generation, more than 80 percent of children grew up in a family with two biological parents who were married to each other. By 1980, only 50 percent could expect to spend their entire childhood in an intact family.[14] Thus:

> The emerging late-20th-century American mind, awash in sensation and cheap sentiment, lurched to the proffered solution. Between 1963 and 1967, all 50 states adopted "reporting laws," requiring doctors, teachers, and social workers to report suspected cases of child abuse. Like Child Saving tools of the past, these laws essentially denied the existence of natural parental rights and the Common Law. Accused parents faced a presumption of guilt (often involving seizure of their children) until they could prove their innocence.[15]

As noted above, the denial of the existence of natural parental rights largely obscured the real cause of child abuse, which was the demise of the intact, autonomous family. Thus, "awash in sensation and cheap sentiment," America "lurched" to a remedy for child abuse that had little if anything to do with the cause.

Today, child abuse seems to be increasing, or at least it is being increasingly identified and reported. Yet the

12

machinery of the child savers is too often directed at the *intact family*—a "special kind of terror unique to the sentimental totalitarianism of late 20th-century America."[16] As George Orwell chillingly forecast, "education" and the ever-vigilant state has begun to scrutinize every family just *in case* there might be child abuse:

The family could not actually be abolished, and, indeed, people were encouraged to be fond of their children in almost the old-fashioned way. The children, on the other hand, were systematically turned against their parents and taught to spy on them and report their deviation. The family had become, in effect, an extension of the Thought Police. It was a device by means of which everyone could be surrounded night and day by informers who knew him intimately.[17]

Lest one believe that George Orwell was an extremist, consider the following case. In Michigan, a public school counselor conducted so-called "counseling" sessions with a young child that included questions such as these: "A girl was listening through the keyhole of the closet door of her parents' bedroom. Here [*sic*] parents were talking and didn't know she was there. What did she hear them saying?"; "What sorts of things are too personal to discuss with your parents?"; "How do you feel after you've gone to the toilet?"; and "What 'turns you on,' that is, what excites you?"[18] In its decision in

13

the lawsuit filed by the parents and The Rutherford Institute to protest such activity by the school, at least to require parental consent for such invasive activities, a federal court said: "[I]t is clear that schools have broad authority to maintain discipline—often at the expense of a student's (and family's) privacy rights."[19] In other words, parents who send their children to public schools risk forfeiting many of the rights heretofore taken for granted.

In contemporary America, social workers, acting at the behest of anonymous tips, pediatricians, emergency room technicians, school teachers, and school friends, may now remove children from their homes essentially at their discretion. Reasons for removing children from their parents include "inadequate parenting skills," "educational neglect" (most often meaning home schooling), "unspecified neglect" (meaning neglect other than shelter neglect, nutritional neglect, medical neglect, or educational neglect); "lack of supervision"; and "emotional abuse or neglect." Many times, these terms simply disguise the real reasons, such as unemployment, lack of adequate income, or substandard housing. Armed with such rationales, the state may take action to rip children from their parents' arms and put them into "temporary" care until a court finds the time to sort things out. Temporary care does not mean two or three days. It usually means years.[20]

Recently, armed force has been added to the scenario. The McDonald family in New York City is a good example. The McDonalds' nightmare began when an anonymous caller contacted the New York City Child Welfare Administration and reported the parents as abusive and neglectful (the allegations rose to the level of concerns such as the children had "bad breath"). The McDonalds are devout Christians who had actively combatted the Rainbow Curriculum in the New York public schools and were now home schooling their children. They had engendered significant animosity and some notoriety for these activities.

The McDonalds insisted that the charges from the anonymous caller were false, but social workers demanded to be let into the family's home to search the children's bodies. Understandably, the McDonalds refused. Incredibly, the social workers returned, only this time they brought *armed* police, ambulances, and men in SWAT uniforms. With a video camera running, Mr. McDonald brought his children to the lobby of his apartment building and asked the sergeant in charge if the children appeared to be in imminent danger. The policeman responded that they did not appear to be in imminent danger and that he would not insist on searching the children in the lobby. In response to a question by Mr. McDonald, one of the policemen said that he *did not care about the constitutional rights of the parents* because he did not want any dead children on his shift. *But no allegations of such danger had been made.*

Unbelievably, the social workers returned to the McDonalds' home a few days later to insist again on being admitted. At that point, the McDonalds fled into hiding with the frightened children and called The Rutherford Institute. A Rutherford Institute staff attorney recognized the seriousness of the situation and, working with attorneys in New York City, immediately obtained a court order restraining these officials from taking further action.

There is little doubt that child abuse, especially sexual child abuse, is increasing. It also seems likely that as numbers of unrelated adults live in homes with children to whom they have no lifetime commitment, these problems will continue to increase. And with increased problems, inevitably the state's presence in our family lives will continue to increase.

Thus, the decline of all freedom in America is inevitably linked to the strength of parental rights and traditional family structures. As author Mary Pride writes:

The root of the problem [sexual child abuse] is social attitudes which disconnect sex from marital responsibility; an increase in unmarried living arrangements and remarriage, with a consequent increase in men living with girls who are not their natural daughters; pornographic propaganda; and the media's desire to cash in on the shock value of child sex. The traditional family stands squarely against all these things. Yet the increase in sexual abuse is being used as an excuse to kick traditional families in the teeth.[21]

Contrary to popular myths, Pride notes:

The home, that is, the *traditional* home of mother, father, and their natural children, is not the cradle of violence. It is the best protection children ever have had, or ever will have. And all the furor over "fighting sexual abuse" looks more like a bid for state control of every family than a sincere attempt to address the problem. The wolf is knocking at the door of the Little Pig's house and crying, "Little Pig, Little Pig, let me come in! I have just finished a study that proves your home is a mess, Little Pig! I have solutions to your problems!" The Little Pig in the story was too smart to believe that a wolf in the house would do him any good.

Are we that smart?[22]

Why Are Traditional Families Declining?

There are many reasons for the declining vitality of America's families. Some of them will be reviewed below.

Not Enough Family Time Together

The most significant adverse effect on modern families is the reduction of time spent together. There are many draws on a family's available time. Cornell University Professor Urie Bronfenbrenner has studied family concerns extensively and writes:

> While the family still has the primary moral and legal responsibility for the character development of children, it often lacks the power or opportunity to do the job, primarily because *parents and children no longer spend enough time together in those situations in which such training is possible.* This is not because parents do not want to spend time with their children. It is simply that conditions have changed.[23]

Like their parents, children are not home much anymore. They leave early on the school bus, and it is close to dinner time when they get back. There may not even be anyone home when they get there:

> If the mother is not working, at least part-time . . . she is out a lot because of social obligations—not just to be with friends, but to do things for the community. The men leave in the morning before the children are up. And they do not get back until after the children have eaten supper. Fathers are often away weekends, as well as during the week.[24]

The State-School

If a child is not with his parents or other adults, where does he spend his time? He or she is with other children —in school, after school, over weekends, and on holidays. School consumes much of the family's time. Mass schooling systems also replaced much of the intellectual richness that developed from an active family life.

Built on the nineteenth-century factory model, mass public education ostensibly taught basic reading, writing, and arithmetic, a bit of theory, and other subjects. However:

> This was the "overt curriculum." But beneath it lay an invisible or "covert curriculum" that was far more basic. It consisted—and still does in most industrial nations—of three courses; one in punctuality, one in obedience, and one in rote, repetitive work. Factory labor demanded workers who showed up on time, especially assembly-line hands. It demanded workers who would take orders from a management hierarchy without questioning. And it demanded men and women prepared to slave away at machines or in offices, performing brutally repetitive operations.[25]

Therefore, from the mid-nineteenth century on, there was a relentless educational progression. American children began school at younger and younger ages; the school year became longer and longer (it climbed 25 percent between 1878 and 1956); and the number of years of compulsory school attendance increased.[26] This has had a profound effect on family patterns:

> By setting up mass education systems, governments not only helped to machine youngsters for their future roles in the industrial work force (hence, in effect, subsidizing industry) but also simultaneously encouraged the spread of the nuclear family form [away from the extended family]. By relieving the family of educational and other traditional functions, governments accelerated the adaptation of family structure to the needs of the factory system.[27]

Mass compulsory school attendance also rigorously promoted a uniform approach to education. With the older one-room schoolhouse, all ages interacted. With mass education, segregation by ages began, and classroom materials and curriculum became standardized. The *diversity* of earlier educational settings and materials was lost.

The mass educational system also produced the professional educator and education bureaucrat. This new type of educator (sometimes referred to as an *educrat*) not only allegedly *knew more* about education, but in the end also *replaced* the parent as the educator of children.

Thus, as a state-financed institution, the public education system began more and more to duplicate, and eventually replace, many family functions *in addition to education.*

However, even this contact is being increasingly restricted. The passing of the neighborhood school in favor of "educational advantages" made possible by consolidation and homogenous grouping by age and more recently by "ability" has set the pattern for other activities. Thus, from preschool days onward, a child's contacts with other children in school, camp, and neighborhood tend to be limited to youngsters of his or her own age and social and/or academic characteristics.

Socialization:
Replaced with Age Segregation

For most of America's history, families socialized their children, albeit unconsciously. Children learned to behave in society from their parents and in the family structure. Today, a *primary function of public schools*, sociologists argue, is to provide for a "uniform orientation at the societal level."[28]

Accordingly, a major role in the *socialization* of America's future citizens has been assumed by the public schools. But mass state schooling has forced children into horizontal peer relationships that have largely displaced the traditional vertical relationships with adults. The result has been a move away from parental relationships to peer relationships along with all the trappings of "peer pressure."

Compulsory public schooling has provided peer groups that occupy a place of primary importance in the life of the student. As Professor James Coleman has noted:

> This setting-apart of our children in schools—which take on ever more functions, ever more "extracurricular activities"—for an ever larger period of training has a singular impact on the child of the high-school age. He is "cut-off" from the rest of society, forced inward toward his own age group, made to carry out his whole social life with others his own age. With his fellows, he comes to constitute a small society, one that has most of its important interactions *within* itself, and maintains only a few threads of connection with the outside adult society.[29]

In essence, this means that the child's primary relationship is no longer parent-child or, for that matter, even child-child. Instead, it is child-state to the extent that the parents' role has been usurped or otherwise filled by the state-controlled public school system.

Because of this aspect of mass compulsory education, America is *moving very rapidly toward a society that is segregated not only by race and class, but also by age.*

Amazingly enough, this age segregation occurs everywhere, even in institutions that formerly encouraged relationships across age lines. Church

Sunday schools, for example, are invariably grouped in such categories as preschool, early grades, teens, singles, young married, adults, senior citizens, and so on. Groupings such as these effectively destroy relationships between younger and older people. Is it any wonder that there is a lack of "community" in churches and Christian groups?

One negative effect of public school socialization is its requirement for conformity. The pressure for conformity to the behavior and beliefs of fellow students is very strong. Sometimes conformity becomes an obsessive drive of students. It almost always has a harmful effect on parent-child relations.

A further negative effect is that the rare nonconforming student who attempts to withstand such socialization pressures is generally, as psychological and sociological studies show, rejected as a deviant or stigmatized in various ways. This can have severe emotional effects on such students when religious beliefs are involved. In fact, one research study indicates that "doubting religious doctrines is the source of much mental anguish and emotional stress on the part of the adolescent."[30]

The religious student, of course, faces this more and more since the full-blown arrival of the so-called, but almost universally misunderstood, separation of church and state doctrine which, as it precluded the state schools from teaching religion, also fragmented the process of education.[31]

The Rutherford Institute regularly handles cases that may appear superficial to those who are not involved. Nonetheless, these cases have a significant impact on the students who are involved, as well as their families. For example, one young student whose paper on the power of God was rejected on the basis of the "separation of church and state," even though the class topic was "The Power of _____," eventually left the state with her family because of the unrelenting torment resulting from her principled resistance and legal action on the matter. The Rutherford Institute has handled numerous cases where an otherwise acceptable and appropriate school paper, project, talent show, or display was censored and disqualified simply because of its Christian content. No Christian detail is too small to be subject to ridicule and censorship in the public schools. For example, in one school a classroom aide removed a tag that said "Jesus Loves You" from the angel costume an elementary school student had worn for the school's Halloween parade. Teenagers who resist the dogma of birth control and abortion in favor of abstinence are too often ridiculed by and ostracized from their school communities.

Alienation

Mass public schooling, along with

the urbanization process and other societal forces, has simply alienated children and parents/adults. For example, one study of 766 sixth-grade children indicated that children, during a weekend, spent an average of two or three hours a day with their parents. During the same period, they spent more time than this with their friends. In short, they spent about twice as much time with peers, either singly or in groups, as with their parents.[32]

Moreover, their behavior apparently reflects preference as well as practice. "When asked with whom they would rather spend a free weekend afternoon," writes Bronfenbrenner, "many more chose friends than parents."[33] However, analysis of the data on the child's perception of his parents, his peers, and himself has led researchers to conclude that "peer-oriented" children were more influenced by a *lack* of attention and concern at home than by the attractiveness of the peer group. "In general, the peer-oriented children held rather negative views of themselves and the peer group. They also expressed a dim view of their own future."[34]

Finally, peer-oriented children report engaging in more antisocial behavior, such as "doing something illegal," "playing hooky," lying, teasing other children, and the like. In summary:

[I]t would seem that the peer-oriented child is more a product of parental disre-

gard than of the attractiveness of the peer group—that he turns to his age-mates less by choice than by default. The vacuum left by the withdrawal of parents and adults from the lives of children is filled with an undesired—and possibly undesirable—substitute of any age-segregated peer group.[35]

No Neighborhoods

The concept of the neighborhood is lost for most Americans. Rarely can a child see people working at their trades. Everyone is out of sight. Children can no longer listen to community talk at the post office or on the park bench. And there are no abandoned houses, no barns, no attics that children may safely explore. It is a bland world for children to grow up in. Forced to remain behind locked doors by the many dangers of an empty home and neighborhood, after-school children whittle away their hours by interacting with their computers and video games. Cyberspace has replaced the neighborhoods familiar to their grandparents.

Families used to be larger—not in terms of more children so much as *more adults.* This included grandparents, uncles, aunts, and cousins. Moreover, those relatives who did not live with the family lived nearby.

There were community visits, dinners, and get-togethers. People knew one another, all of them—the old folks, the middle-aged, the older cousins.

And what's more, they knew everyone else. This had its good side and its bad side:

> One the good side, some of these relatives were interesting people, or so you thought at the time. Uncle Charlie had been to China. Aunt Sue made the best penuche fudge on the block. Cousin Bill could read people's minds (he claimed). And they all gave you presents.

> But there was the other side. You had to give them all Christmas presents. Besides, everybody minded your business. They wanted to know where you had been, where you were going, and why. And if they did not like what they heard, they said so (particularly if you had told the truth).[36]

The stable world of the small town has been absorbed by an ever-shifting suburbia. As a consequence, children are growing up today in a different kind of environment. Urbanization has reduced the extended family to a nuclear, atomistic one *with only two adults.* The functioning neighborhood —where it has not decayed into an urban or rural slum—has withered to a small circle of friends, most of them accessible only by car or telephone. Paradoxically, although there are more people around, *there are fewer opportunities for meaningful human contact.*

Whereas previously the world in which the child lived consisted of a diversity of people in a diversity of settings, now, for millions of American children, the neighborhood is nothing but row upon row of buildings where "other people" live. One house or apartment is much like another—and so are the people. As Professor Bronfenbrenner writes:

> They all have more or less the same income, and the same way of life. But the child does not see much of that life, for all that people do in the neighborhood is to come home to it, have a drink, eat dinner, mow the lawn, watch television, and sleep. Increasingly often, today's housing projects have no stores, no shops, no services, no adults at work or play. This is the sterile world in which many of our children grow, and this is the "urban renewal" we offer to the families we would rescue from the slums.[37]

This is a by-product of a variety of changes, all operating to decrease the prominence and power of the family in the lives of children. These social changes include "[u]rbanization, child labor laws, the abolishment of the apprentice system, commuting, centralized schools, zoning ordinances, the working mothers, the experts' advice to be permissive, the seductive power of television for keeping children occupied, the delegation and professionalization of child care."[38]

All of these manifestations of "progress" have operated to decrease opportunities of contact between children and parents or, for that matter, adults in general. As a result, *parents and children have become strangers.*

Thus, over the years, the decline in family vitality has resulted in a shift of responsibility for the upbringing of children away from the family to other settings in the society—such as schools and state and private institutions and individuals who attempt to simulate the original family setting (for example, foster parents).

The State as Parent

As discussed above, the shift in responsibility for children away from the family inevitably brings state intervention.

It is evident that the Judeo-Christian worldview affected English jurisprudence concerning parental rights and the early development of the law on parental rights in America. These early views tolerated state interference only where it was *clear* that the parents had forfeited their rights.[39]

However, the modern child savers demand that parents who have had their children taken away be required to provide "concrete evidence of their positive motivation toward being a parent and the steps they are taking in that direction, *before* they get their children back."[40]

Essentially, the child savers have shifted the burden of proof to the parents to prove they are fit, rather than require the state to prove they are unfit. In other words, instead of "innocent until proven guilty," the standard is now "guilty until proven innocent." All too often, the social welfare bureaucracies include legitimate parental actions, such as nonabusive corporal punishment, within their range of concerns. A witch-hunt mentality prevails that marks *all* parents as suspected child abusers. This ranges from the social worker who investigates suspected child abuse to the lawmaker crafting abuse legislation.

According to Dr. Richard A. Gardner, a clinical professor of child psychiatry at Columbia University and an expert on the sexual abuse of children, the basic problem with child abuse legislation is that the system is indeed biased.[41] Dr. Gardner has this to say:

> State and Federal money is available for the treatment of children who are found to have been abused, but no funds have been specifically allocated for the protection and treatment of those who have been falsely accused. Nor has money been available for another special and growing group— children who have suffered psychiatric disturbances because they have been used as vehicles for the promulgation of a false accusation. . . . Evaluators who conclude there has been abuse set in motion events that bring their offices both state and federal funds. If they conclude there was no abuse, their facilities receive no funding for further evaluation of treatment.[42]

The current system generates an endless stream of referrals for investigators and "validators." All this predictably fuels child abuse hysteria, hysteria in which an accused individual's constitutional due process protections and parental rights are commonly ignored.[43]

In this respect, all fifty states and the District of Columbia have passed mandatory reporting laws, and most of these require reporting of suspected child abuse by physicians, educators, psychologists, and others likely to come in contact with children.[44] The level of suspicion that triggers the reporting duty is less than probable cause.[45] Most statutes use words such as "reasonable cause to believe," "cause to believe," or "known or suspected abuse."[46] The statutes of all jurisdictions provide some immunity from civil or criminal liability for those who, in good faith, report suspected abuse or neglect.[47]

Thus, as an example, in 1991, 49,163 children in Virginia were the subjects of investigation for child abuse or neglect.[48] Of those cases, 13,894 were "founded" or were "reason to suspect" child abuse cases. The rest, 35,269, were "unfounded"; that is, the social worker found no reason to believe that abuse or neglect occurred.[49]

As one report recognizes, for the families represented in the 35,269 "unfounded" cases, and thus needlessly investigated by social workers, "it was

31

an embarrassing and complex web of administrative formulas, perceptions and questions about their parental skills."[50]

The child savers have even been allowed to "justify state intervention not just in cases of real abuse but even when the choice is only between *good* and *better* environments for a child."[51]

The result of these combined influences is a frightening increase of cases where parents are erroneously accused of abusing their children. As a consequence, children are taken away from their parents, and the entire family is emotionally ravaged, perhaps irreparably destroyed, by state legal mechanisms.

The Children's Revolution: What Lies Ahead

Until recently, the child savers operated largely on the premise of *parens patriae* (*i.e.*, the state acting as the parent). The state, operating through its child savers, usurped traditional family responsibilities or convinced families to delegate their duties to the state.

Today, the demise of parents' rights, and thus the rights of families, is shifting into its final phase. Momentum is growing for the notion that children should have rights that they may assert independently of either their parents or the state acting on their behalf.

Thus, today's child savers are promoting legislation that will institutionalize such rights. On an international level, this may be seen in the proposed United Nations Convention on the Rights of the Child.

The Convention on the Rights of the Child[52] was adopted by the United Nations General Assembly without vote on November 20, 1989. The treaty contains a number of human rights that have never before been protected in an international treaty—including many new *rights* for children. The primary consideration of the convention is to promote "the best interests of the child,"[53] a commendable goal. However, several provisions in the treaty appear to undermine parental authority.

The treaty contains some radical concepts for parents in the United States, and the debate regarding this convention is important. Ideas that become familiar have a way of becoming accepted. However, even if the United Nations Convention on the Rights of the Child is ratified by the United States, the constitutional rights of parents would, under present law, supersede the treaty.

First, Article VI of the United States Constitution (the "Supremacy Clause") says that:

> This Constitution, and the Laws of the United States which shall be made in Pursuance thereof; and all Treaties made, or which shall be made, under the Authority of the United States, shall be the supreme Law of the Land;

and the Judges in every State shall be bound thereby, any Thing in the Constitution [of a State] or the Laws of any State to the Contrary notwithstanding.[54]

The Supremacy Clause places all state laws and constitutions under the authority of the federal Constitution, as well as under that of any treaty to which the United States is a party. Thus, while treaties that are signed by the United States will override any conflicting state legislation, the Supremacy Clause places the Constitution of the United States and such treaties on an equal plane.[55] *Both* documents are to be viewed as the "supreme Law of the Land."[56]

The question of which document prevails if a treaty contradicts certain provisions in the Constitution is answered by numerous decisions of the Supreme Court, the most notable of which is *Reid v. Covert*.[57] In this case, the Supreme Court said:

> It would be manifestly contrary to the objectives of those who crafted the Constitution, as well as those who were responsible for the Bill of Rights—let alone alien to our entire constitutional history and tradition—to construe Article VI as permitting the United States to exercise power under an international agreement without observing constitutional prohibitions.[58]

The opinion of the Supreme Court in this case emphasizes further that "this

Court has regularly and uniformly recognized the supremacy of the Constitution over a treaty."[59]

In *Asakura v. Seattle*[60] and *Missouri v. Holland*,[61] the Supreme Court said that even though the treaty-making power of the United States does not extend "so far as to authorize what the Constitution forbids, it does extend to all proper subjects of negotiation between our government and other nations."[62] Thus, the question arises as to whether issues of parental authority and child autonomy are proper subjects of negotiation since the Constitution grants parental rights regarding the upbringing of children.

Parental liberty and authority over the upbringing of children has long been recognized by the Supreme Court as a *fundamental right* under the Constitution. The Court stated in the 1972 case of *Wisconsin v. Yoder* that "this primary role of the parents in the upbringing of their children is now established beyond debate as an enduring American tradition."[63] The Ohio Supreme Court similarly stated in 1976: "Thus, it has long been recognized that the right of a parent to guide the education, including the religious education, of his or her children is indeed a 'fundamental right.'"[64]

Another important Supreme Court case recognizing parental liberty to be of greater import than any authority which the State may have over children is *Pierce v. Society of Sisters.*[65] In Pierce, the Supreme Court held that "[t]he child is not the mere creature of the State; those who nurture him and direct his destiny have the right, coupled with the high duty, to recognize and prepare him for additional obligations."[66]

Thus, established precedent shows that the Constitution would supersede any contradictory treaty. *If* the convention should be adopted by the United States, any provisions deemed to contradict parental rights granted under the Constitution would be void.

For these and other more technical reasons, there are significant obstacles to the United Nations Convention on the Rights of the Child becoming the law of the land in the United States. However, what is *very significant* about this convention is the fact that it is being discussed at all! Contrasted with the high esteem in which American families were held at this country's birth, the fact that this convention would *even be discussed* is clear and convincing evidence of the decline of respect for parental rights.

This decline is further demonstrated by the work of organizations such as the Children's Defense Fund. Hillary Rodham Clinton, wife of President Bill Clinton, has been a board member of the Children's Defense Fund which, among other things, advocates giving children the standing to sue their parents.[67] Mrs. Clinton has been quoted as saying that "children should have a right to be permitted to decide their own futures."[68]

Hillary Clinton is not just referring to children who are abused and neglected. She also refers to such matters as "abortion, schooling, cosmetic surgery, employment, and others where the decision or lack of one will significantly affect the children's future."[69] An article in the October 19, 1992, issue of the *National Review* documents this view:

In Mrs. Clinton's world, there will be a children's rights bar, legal counselors in the junior high schools, a growing library of legal treatises on juvenile rights, five-part Supreme Court tests for determining which parental decisions "significantly affect" children's futures, Ivy League law-review essays on youthful self-esteem and the due process clause, and bipartisan congressional initiatives to enforce the latest judicial emanation on the entitlement of children.

The social impact of all this will be subtle in the same way that the social impact of earlier legal revolutions in obscenity, school prayer, abortion, welfare, and divorce has been subtle. The state will have a basis for wanting to know more about the family life of children, third parties will be encouraged to intrude more quickly, and parental authority will be eroded as such practices as corporal punishment and restrictions on social relationships are questioned throughout well-publicized lawsuits.[70]

According to Mrs. Clinton: "The law is not unresponsive to societal values, and decisions are frequently influenced by notions of conventional morality, occasionally reflecting acceptance of changing morality."[71]

In a society that protects a minor's "right" to an abortion, provides birth control and sex education over parental objections, and mandates state education heading toward affective outcomes, what could be left for Mrs. Clinton to give our children?

Mrs. Clinton has herself proposed several very specific ways to "resolve the theoretical problems" arising out of parental control of their children:

First, the "legal status of infancy, or minority, should be abolished and the presumption of incompetency reversed."

Second, all "procedural rights guaranteed to adults under the Constitution should be granted to children whenever the state or a third party moves against them, judicially or administratively" (third parties, remember, include *parents)*.

Finally, the "presumption of identity of interests between parents and their children should be rejected whenever the child has interests demonstrably independent of those of his parents (as determined by the *consequences* for both the parents and the child of the action in question), and a competent child should be permitted to assert his or her own interests."[72]

This agenda of Mrs. Clinton and others may well be reflected in the governmental policies and court decisions of the 1990s and far beyond.

Are Things Better?

There is little doubt that the traditional two-parent family adhering to Judeo-Christian principles provides stable and productive children.[73] The demise of such families and the surrender of family responsibilities to the state are largely to blame for the decline in economic conditions and education and the rise in teen suicide, teen pregnancy, abortion, and crime. Thus:

> According to a growing body of social-scientific evidence, children in families disrupted by divorce and out-of-wedlock birth do worse than children in intact families on several measures of well-being. Children in single-parent families are six times as likely to be poor. A 1988 survey by the National Center for Health Statistics found children in single-parent families to have emotional and behavioral problems. They are also more likely to drop out of high school, to get pregnant as teenagers, to abuse drugs, and to be in trouble with the law. Compared with children in two-parent families, children from disrupted families are at a much higher risk for physical or sexual abuse.

Overall child well-being has declined, despite a decrease in the number of children per family, an increase in the educational level of parents, and historically high levels of public spending. After dropping in the 1960s and 1970s, the proportion of children in poverty has increased dramatically, from 15 percent in 1970 to 20 percent in 1990, while the percentage of adult Americans in poverty has remained roughly constant. The teen suicide rate has more than tripled. Juvenile crime has increased and become more violent. School performance has continued to decline. There are no signs that these trends are about to reverse themselves.

If we fail to come to terms with the relationship between family structure and the declining child well-being, then it will be increasingly difficult to improve children's life prospects, no matter how many new programs the federal government funds. Nor will we be able to make progress in bettering school performance or reducing crime or improving the quality of the nation's future work force—all domestic problems closely connected to family breakup. Worse, we may contribute to the problems by pursuing policies that actually increase family instability and breakup.[74]

There is not much doubt that many of America's children are in trouble. There is little doubt that many of America's families and parents are in trouble.

One thing is clear, however. The family will not revive overnight. It will take work based on love and compassion, so often missing in the family setting.

Barbara Bush summed it up well: "Our success as a society depends not on what happens in the White House but inside your house."[75]

Inside Our Houses

If there is to be any recovery of the basic values that give form and freedom to society and provide worth and dignity to individuals, it will originate from healthy families. In this respect, Christians in particular must take a close look at how their families function.

True Christianity starts at home. Christians, as should be obvious, can evangelize the world; but if they are neglecting their families in the process then, at least personally, their work is for naught. Evangelization and love for your fellow creature, therefore, begin in the family unit.

If Christians are consistently to speak and stand for the truth, it will be due not only to core beliefs but also to a strong, undergirding family structure. The need is therefore great to revitalize the biblical family structure. This need does not deny the reality that many contemporary homes have no traditional family structure, with perhaps only one, or no, parent present. However, as Christians, we must never concede the biblical ideal. This

41

means that all families, no matter how they are configured, should emulate the biblical ideal to the maximum extent possible.

Functions

Historically and biblically, the family is the central institution in society, with obvious procreative functions. Ideally, believers marry because they share a bond of faith and love and resolve to maintain this bond for life under God. They thus create a family system that cannot be duplicated by either science or imagination as the ideal institution for raising children.

There are many reasons why the family is the foundational institution of a free society. First and foremost, the family should be society's basic health and welfare institution, caring for and educating its own without any outside compulsion.[76] When the family begins to break down, however, the state assumes the basic health, welfare, and education functions and generally does an ineffective job. And there is no possibility that the state can fully replace the parental function; hence, the state's performance as "family" will always be deficient and, inevitably, coercive.

The family is a person's first school, and parents are the educators, performing the most difficult of all educational tasks, teaching the child to speak. This is an important task, but it comes simply and naturally in the family as the result of a parent's love and the child's response to that love.

Self-Government

The family is also the first government in the life of a child. Within the family setting, children should learn self-government, motivation, and guidance. Again, this flows naturally from the parents' natural love for their children. The children thus receive the highest order of motivation.

In a biblically structured family, the father will serve as the head of the household. He is the authority within the family relationship. The Bible is very clear, however, that the father should not be a dictator. Parents and children, therefore, learn from, and are governed by, the biblical family model.

The father is governed by the necessities of providing for the family, protecting family members, and giving them the example and leadership they need. Conversely, a father who will not provide for his family will not be respected and will have neither the authority nor the ability to govern with wisdom and honor. The Bible states clearly that if anyone does not provide for his own, especially those of his own household, "he has denied the faith and is worse than an unbeliever."[77] In the biblical model, the mother is voluntarily governed in her activities by the requirements of her husband and children.

Spousal Love

Other biblical injunctions deal with a current problem in the church. Many Christian men, unfortunately, imprison their wives in the house and treat them like slaves. This runs counter to the high estate placed upon women in the Bible and, in particular, to the reverent relationship men are to have with women.

The Proverbs 31 "virtuous wife" is a good example of how God views women. This chapter of the Bible clearly indicates that women (including wives) are to be afforded a great deal of respect. For example, in Proverbs 31:16, the wife owns property and acts as a business person. This biblical view runs counter to the way women are often viewed in Christian circles today.

Husbands, both Christian and non-Christian, need to reevaluate their relationship with their wives. A necessary element in the spousal relationship is the attention and love shown by the husband toward his wife. Indeed, the husband is to love his wife "just as Christ loved the church and gave himself up for her."[78] Men are also to love their wives "as their own bodies."[79] Failure to do so will interfere with God's blessing on that family.

A trend among so-called evangelical circles is the emphasis on male-male and female-female relationships, especially between married persons. Thus, large auditoriums are filled with Christian men who are "bonding" with each other and forming relationships that may supplant, or at least supersede, those with their wives. Similarly, some Christian organizations are exhorting married women to form relationships with other women so that they can work out the problems in their daily lives. These movements can be anti-marriage and antifamily in many ways. After one's relationship with God, *no relationship should be more intimate or more important than that of husband and wife*. To form such relationships may ultimately undermine the marriage and the family relationships.

The Education Factor

A basic function of parents that must be recovered from the state is *education*. The assembly-line education of both the state and private (including Christian) schools must be rethought.

The idea that only "professional" educators are qualified to teach children is a myth perpetrated by the educational establishment. Another more absurd myth is the concept that teachers must be certified by the state in order to be qualified to teach. The men and women who built America, for example, were essentially home taught by either their "uncertified, nonprofessional" parents or tutors who assisted their parents.

The family can recover the education function. In some ways, this is happening today. It is primarily happening through the growing home school movement and "parent-run" private schools.

Christian schools that are not parent-run are falling into the same trap as the state schools in usurping the function of the family. This can be easily remedied by putting parents in control of the school. This does not mean merely having parent meetings at the school. It means having parents on the school board and heavily involved in every aspect of the school. Otherwise, even private Christian schools can tend to be antiparent.

If at all possible, Christian and other private schools should cooperate with those parents teaching their children in the home. Christian schools can allow home-education parents the use of their facilities as well as allow home-education children to take certain courses of instruction at the school.

Also, compulsory school attendance laws should be revised to allow children to spend fewer hours in formal schooling. *Children should be encouraged to spend more time at home with their parents.* There is much "dead time" during the school day, and, if this could be eliminated, less time at the school building would be required.

Human Contact

Children need people in order to reach their full human potential. Isolation of children from adults simultaneously threatens the growth of the individual and the survival of society. *Child-rearing is not something children can do for themselves.* As one noted authority recognizes:

> It is primarily through observing, playing, and working with others older and younger than himself that a child discovers both what he can do and who he can become—that he develops both his ability and his identity. It is primarily through exposure and interaction with adults and children of different ages that a child acquires new interests and skills and learns the meaning of tolerance, cooperation, and compassion. Hence to relegate children to a world of their own is to deprive them of their humanity, and ourselves as well.[80]

What we are experiencing is a breakdown in the process of making human beings human. "By isolating our children from the rest of society, we abandon them to a world devoid of adults and ruled by the destructive impulses and controlling pressures both of the age-segregated peer group and the aggressive and exploitative television screen. We leave our children bereft of standards and support and our own lives impoverished and corrupted."[81]

Many have simply reversed their priorities. Other things have become more important than children. This is a betrayal of our children. It underlines the ever-increasing disillusionment and alienation among young people in all segments of society.

Those who grew up in a setting where children and families were respected are able to react to the frustrations of modern secular society in positive ways. Parents and families are a part of their lives.

However, those who came from situations in which families and children were a low priority are striking out. The alienated child, for whatever reason, sets up his or her parents and society as objects of resistance.

Thus, it is the family that builds productive people. This means, again, that parents and children must be together. It also means that *parents and children should be with each other in the family setting as much as possible.*

Consequently, parents should do what some may consider to be old-fashioned, that is, *keep their children at home,* away from all the extracurricular activities that tend to disrupt families today.

On the other hand, parents must keep themselves within the family environment. Fathers and mothers who are workaholics are not good parents.

All current trends point to the increasing participation of women and *mothers* in the work force. One may dispute whether women are more gifted and effective in the care of young children than are men. However, the fact remains that in today's society the care of our children depends overwhelmingly on women, and mothers in particular.

Contrary to what many may assert, the most important function any woman serves is that of being a mother. Children deprived of a mother for any reason are children who have been robbed. There should be no "latchkey" children. The child must have the security that only a mother can give.

There are instances where it is necessary for mothers to work. If so, there are numerous in-home employment opportunities for mothers; or fathers and mothers who wish to be close to their children could both work out of the home and split the work hours. Part-time work for mothers is another option.

There is one caveat, however. Mothers with *small* children should avoid working outside the home. Mothers often have their greatest impact on young children. And small children need mother contact in their early years.

With the withdrawal of societal support of the family, women and mothers have become more isolated.

An increasing responsibility for the care and upbringing of children has fallen on the young mother. Under some circumstances, it is not surprising that many young women in America are in the process of revolting.

If parents do not begin to increase the time they spend with their children, the "alienation gap" is going to increase. As a result, children will become even more estranged. Simply put, it is much easier to assert children's rights against parents who are strangers.

A family is built upon human relationships. It takes effort and *time* on the part of parents to develop relationships with their children. It means taking *time* with children, reading aloud to them, playing with them, working with them, shopping with them, and so forth. This builds relationships.

Children are the living messages we send to a time we will not see. They are the combined images of their parents. They must, therefore, be molded with love and compassion.

The Television Trap

Children must be guarded and protected but not shielded altogether from reality. Reality, like strong medicine, though, must come in small doses. Too much reality too soon obliterates the distinctions between children and adults. This brings us to the subject of television.

The Nielsen surveys of American viewers reveal that the average family watches television seven hours a day. "This has never happened before in history. No people has ever been entertained for seven hours a *day*."[82]

Television, besides consuming precious time, invades the privacy of the home. It almost always teaches an ethic that runs contrary to the foundation of the traditional family. It is, then, a very subtle (although sometimes overt) attack on the family.

One Michigan State University study in the early 1980s offered a group of four- and five-year-olds the choice of giving up television or their fathers. One-third of the group said they would give up their fathers.[83]

Obviously, television has had a devastating impact on the American culture. It is a dominating force that alters behavior. Author Pete Hamill notes:

> Viewers can't work or play while watching television; they can't read; they can't be out on the streets, falling in love with the wrong people, learning how to quarrel and compromise with other human beings. In short, they are asocial. So are drug addicts.[84]

Hamill continues:

> In short, television works on the same imaginative and intellectual level as psychoactive drugs. If prolonged television viewing makes the young passive (dozens of studies indicate that it

does), then moving to drugs has a certain coherence. Drugs provide an unearned high (in contrast to the earned rush that comes from a feat accomplished, a human breakthrough earned by sweat or thought or love).[85]

Christians must participate in the real world. They should not deprive their children altogether of a cultural reality such as television. Disposing of the television set will not make it disappear. Monitoring it can, in large part, tame it.

"As a beginning," writes author Pete Hamill, "parents must take immediate control of the sets, teaching children to watch specific *programs*, not 'television,' to get out of the house and play with other kids. Elementary and high schools must begin teaching television as a subject, the way literature is taught, showing children how shows are made, how to distinguish between the true and the false, and how to recognize cheap emotional manipulation. All Americans should spend more time reading. And thinking.[86]

These principles also apply to "Christian" programs as well. Because of its manipulative nature, much of so-called Christian programming is not healthy for adults or children (any more than secular programming is).

Television is also an intruder that prevents family unity. Many television programs and commercials are highly destructive to young minds. They eschew moral judgments and program viewers only to buy products. In the realm of the commercial, nothing is sacred.

Videotapes provide a good alternative to regular television fare. There are many good movies and educational videotapes that are both enjoyable and instructive.

The best way to watch television is as a family, which allows both parental critique and interplay with the children in discussing the content. Television should never serve as a baby-sitter. Intentional or not, television is a teacher, and, if not controlled, is a teacher of the worst sort.

Creativity and Interaction

Christian endeavors in the arts are in a dismal state. The biblical and traditional view of the arts and creativity as gifts of God have largely been discarded. However, any Christian revitalization in terms of the arts will begin in the family. It is here that parental direction and guidance could help produce an entirely new generation of artists.

Christians need to emerge from their evangelical ghettos and acquire the ability to understand and discuss the arts intelligently. This does not mean that they should be absorbed with the respective works or subjects, nor does it mean that the Christian should necessarily approve of the content. It simply means that the believer should be able to interpret art and art forms in terms of their ideas and underlying ethos and respond in the appropriate way. The arts, after all, often indicate the direction in which a society is heading. For example, Picasso's work effectively foretold an era of mass inhumanity.

In terms of entertainment, Christians should disabuse themselves of the notion that all rock music or all movies are evil. Christians must not be flippant condemners of everything but should be able to praise what is good, even if they do not agree with the lifestyle of the artist or the content of the message.

For example, one may not agree with the point of view of a particular film but may still recognize merit in technical aspects, such as direction, cinematography, and so on. At the same time, however, one must be careful not to allow brilliant cinematography to seduce one into accepting an anti-Christian message. Moreover, one may not be fond of jazz but should be able to appreciate the skills of jazz musicians.

While all Christians should be able to interpret the arts, some will want to be participants. And there is no good reason why they should not. Indeed, there is every reason why they should. Artistic creativity is a gift of God. As such, it is the imagination of the Christian that should soar beyond the stars.

Just as the arts need no justification, Christian participation in them needs no justification. Involvement in the arts cannot be opposed on the grounds that the world is divided into "spiritual" and "secular" spheres. As it happens, the word *secular* does not appear in the Bible.

There is much that a family can do in the way of becoming involved in the arts. The key is parental participation. Homes can be decorated with inexpensive prints of some of the great artists, such as Rembrandt, Raphael, Matisse, and others. Homes become, in effect, art galleries.

Parents should take time to listen to music with their children. This should include all types of music, from classical to modern music. Parents should teach their children to take art seriously and be able to evaluate it through a Judeo-Christian worldview. If this type of instruction is not done with children, they too often will avoid the arts completely or tend to be ignorant of what they are listening to and/or viewing.

Role of the Church

The properly functioning Christian family is the central source of power and social energy in any society.

Because the Christian family is the great locale of power, it has often incurred the enmity of other claimants to power. One of those has been the church.

The older asceticism, because of misinterpretation of certain "celibacy" passages in the Bible, saw marital life as a lower way of life and, at times, showed no little hostility toward the family. This attitude is still present in many evangelical churches in a disguised form. The family is, in effect, "saved" from itself by being drawn into the church night after night for church activities. At one time, for example, church elders made annual visitation to all homes to ensure that the children were taught their catechism and that family prayer and Bible study were the practice. Today, the effort is directed toward attendance at weekday church prayer meetings and Bible study. The center, therefore, has shifted.

However, the center should be returned to the family. The local church should stress the importance of the family (and, therefore, the home) as *the* center of worship, education, and development of human beings—that is, the center of power. This in turn will have the effect of decentralizing society in general.

The church and pastor must loosen their authoritarian control over parishioners and especially families. This will mean decreasing activities that tear parents and children away from the home.

These principles should be taught in the local church. Moreover, the church as a teaching institution should provide families with the necessary instruction and educational materials on developing strong families. Therefore, a central effort of local churches should be to build up families.

Contrary to what some may think, this will not weaken local churches. In fact, the opposite is true. Strong families make strong churches.

The entire "jet-setting" mentality of modern Christianity is harmful. The evangelists and Christian celebrities who have families and are on the road more than they are at home with their wives and children are not doing the Lord's work in the truest sense. The basic ministry of a father and a mother is the family. Saving the world but losing your children is a heavy price to pay for fulfillment of big egos. It hurts everyone.

Priorities are thus the key. Do we want to be with our families, or do we want to attend the endless string of "Christian" seminars and conferences that too often occur on weekends (when parents should be with their children)?

Strangers in the Land

The Bible commands us: "Honor your father and your mother, so that you *may live long in the land* the Lord your God is giving you."[87]

If Christian parents and adults will commit themselves to the support of strong families based upon traditional Judeo-Christian principles, then the children, who have become strangers in the land, will return.

If this is not done, society will continue to atomize, and the power of the state will continue to grow and threaten our rights as parents and, ultimately, our very rights to life and liberty.

As those who call themselves Christians look into the cold eyes of their children, who are completely estranged and battle their parents and others, remember that there may have been a time when this confrontation could have been avoided. As we look into the eyes of the professional "parent," who bears the imprimatur of the state as he or she overrides the parental rights given by God and enshrined in the Constitution, remember that there may have been a time when this could have baeen avoided.

To do so requires commitment—commitment to people in pursuing a better future for all of God's children. The starting point is in your own home.

Notes

1. *See generally,* John W. Whitehead, *Religious Apartheid* (Chicago, Ill.: Moody, 1994).
2. Allan Carlson, "Uncle Sam's Child," *Chronicles* (January 1993), 12–13.

3. *DeBurgh v. DeBurgh*, 39 Cal. 2d 858, 863–64, 250 P.2d 598, 601 (1952).

In *Moore v. East Cleveland*, 431 U.S. 494 (1973), the formulation of protected freedoms were those that are "deeply rooted in this Nation's history and tradition" *(id., citing Moore*, 431 U.S. at 503). As was earlier noted, the common law structure also relied on history and tradition to protect parental rights. A basic reason for classifying parental rights as fundamental is the presumption that parents have innate affection for their children and are the adults most able to determine the child's best interests and the means of protecting those interests *(Parham v. J.R.*, 442 U.S. 584, 601–04 (1979), and cases cited therein). Although the holding in Parham recognizes strong parental rights, the case does not explicitly characterize parents' rights as fundamental.

4. Barbara DaFoe Whitehead, "Dan Quayle Was Right," *The Atlantic Monthly* 271, no. 4 (April 1993), 84 (italics added).

5. *See generally*, R. Collin Mangrum, *Religious Constraints During Visitation: Under What Circumstances Are They Constitutional?*, 24 CREIGHTON LAW REVIEW 445 (1991).

6. *Ibid.*, 474. *See also* J. Rawls, *A Theory of Justice* (Cambridge: Harvard Univ. Press, 1971).

7. Carlson, "Uncle Sam's Child," 13.

8. *Ibid.*

9. *Ibid.*

10. *Ibid.*

11. *Ibid.*

12. *Ibid.*

13. *Ibid.*, 13–14.

14. Barbara DaFoe Whitehead, "Dan Quayle Was Right," 47.

15. Carlson, "Uncle Sam's Child," 14.

16. *Ibid.*

17. George Orwell, *Nineteen Eighty-Four* (New York: Harcourt, Brace, World, 1949), 136–37.

18. *Newkirk v. East Lansing Schools*, No. 1:91: CV: 563 (U.S. Dist. Ct., W.D. Mich.), 1993.

19. *Id.* at 13.

20. *See* Mary Pride, *The Child Abuse Industry* (Westchester, Ill.: Crossway, 1989).

21. *Ibid.*

22. *Ibid.*

23. Urie Bronfenbrenner, *Two Worlds of Childhood: U.S. and U.S.S.R.* (New York: Russell Sage Foundation, 1970), 95.

24. *Ibid.*

25. Alvin Toffler, *The Third Wave* (New York: William Morrow, 1980), 45.

26. *Ibid.*

27. *Ibid.*, 81.

28. Havy C. Bredemeier and Richard M. Stephenson, *The Analysis of Social Systems* (New York: Holt, Rinehart, & Winston, 1962), 119.

29. James Coleman, *The Adolescent Society* (New York: Free Press of Glencoe, 1961), 3 (italics in original).

30. Elizabeth Hurlock, *Child Development* (New York: McGraw-Hill, 1942), 359.

31. *See generally*, John W. Whitehead, *The Rights of Religious Persons in Public Education*, rev. ed. (Wheaton, Ill.: Crossway, 1994).

32. Bronfenbrenner, *Two Worlds of Childhood*, 101.

33. *Ibid.*

34. *Ibid.*

35. *Ibid.*, 102 (italics, in part, supplied).

36. *Ibid.*, 96.

37. *Ibid.*, 97.

38. *Ibid.*, 99.

39. A nineteenth-century English court explained the justification for judicial interference in parental authority:

> A father has a legal right to control and direct the education and bringing up of his children until they attain the age of twenty-one years ... and the Court will not interfere with him in the exercise of his paternal authority, except (1) where by his gross moral turpitude he forfeits his rights, or (2) where he has by his conduct abdicated his parental authority.

In re Agar-Ellis, 24 Ch. D. 3l7 (Ca.) (1993). In the 1982 decision of *Santosky v. Kramer*, 455 U.S. 745 (1982), the critical issue of burden of proof in parental rights termination hearings was argued. The statute in New York required a "fair preponderance of the evidence," and a 5-4 majority held this standard to be unconstitutionally low. The Court imposed a "clear and convincing evidence" standard as a Fourteenth Amendment norm. *Id.*

40. Karen Dorros, Ph.D., and Patricia Dorsey, "Whose Rights Are We Protecting Anyway?" *Children Today* (May-June 1989), 8.

41. Dr. Richard A. Gardner, "Modern Witch Hunt—Child Abuse Charges," *The Wall Street Journal* (22 February 1993), A, 10:3.

42. *Ibid.*

43. *Ibid.*

44. John E. B. Myers, "A Survey of Child Abuse and Neglect Reporting Statutes," 10 THE JOUN. OF JUVENILE LAW 1, at 4 (1986).

45. *Roman v. Appleby*, 558 F. Supp. 449, 459 (E.D. Pa. 1983).

46. *See* Myers, "A Survey of Child Abuse and Neglect Reporting Statutes," 4.

47. *Ibid.*, 6.

48. Ophelia D. Johnson, "Parents Feel Besieged by Suspicions," *Richmond Times-Dispatch* (3 May 1992), A-11.

49. *Ibid.*

50. *Ibid.*

51. Carlson, "Uncle Sam's Child," 18 (italics added).

52. Convention on the Rights of the Child, G.A. Res. 44/25, U.N. GAOR Annex, U.N. Doc. A/44/736 (1989), reprinted in 28 "Int'l Legal Materials," 1456 (1990).

53. *The United Nations Convention on the Rights of the Child,* Art. 3, Sec. 1 (1989).

54. U.S. Const., Art. VI, Sec. 1, Cl.2.

55. *Ibid.*

56. *Ibid.*

57. 354 U.S. 1 (1956).

58. *Id.* at 17.

59. *Id. See also U.S. v. Minnesota,* 270 U.S. 181, 207–8 (1926); *Holden v. Joy,* 84 U.S. 211, 17 Wall. 211, 242–43 (1872); *The Cherokee Tobacco,* 78 U.S. 616, 11 Wall. 616, 620–21 (1870); *Doe v. Braden,* 57 U.S. 635, 16 How. 635, 657 (1853); *cf. Marbury v. Madison,* 5 U.S. 137, 1 Cranch 137, 176–80 (1803).

60. 265 U.S. 332 (1924).

61. 252 U.S. 416 (1920).

62. 265 U.S. at 341.

63. 406 U.S. 205, 232 (1972).

64. *State v. Whisner,* 47 Ohio St. 2d 181 (1976). *Accord, e.g., In re Pierce,* 451 A.2d 363, 367 (1982) (concurring opinion; *Perchemlides v. Frizzle,* No. 16641, slip op. at 6 (Mass. Super. Cit., Hampshire County, Nov. 13, 1978); *Stanley v. Illinois,* 405 U.S. 645 (1972).

65. 268 U.S. 510 (1925).

66. *Id.* at 535. *See also Meyer v. Nebraska,* 262 U.S. 390, 399 (1923).

67. "Divorce, Clinton-Style," *National Review* (19 October 1992), 18.

68. *Ibid.*

69. *Ibid.*